Online Marketing

Online Media Planning
Pay Per Click Search Marketing
Organic Search Engine Optimization
Email Marketing
Affiliate Marketing
Rich Media & Banner Advertising
Viral Marketing
Social Networks, Blogs & RSS
Analytics

This edition published 2006

Imano plc	Imano inc
198 High Holborn	27 West 20th Street
London WC1V 7BD	New York 10011
United Kingdom	USA
Telephone: 020 7632 6930	Telephone: 646 442 4416
Email: experts@imano.com	Email: us.experts@imano.com
www.imano.com	www.imano.com

ISBN 0-9549055-3-9

Contents

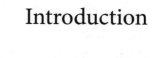

Introduction

Introduction

Online marketing has seen a substantial growth over the past 5 years with spending predicted to reach \$23bn in the US by 2010[1]. Compared to TV and radio, online marketing is a relatively new medium and there is substantial experimentation as companies learn what works for them and the industry as a whole. Online marketing has a level of immediacy, personalization and accountability that much traditional media is unable to deliver. Newer channels such as search engine marketing are changing the marketing landscape as traditional agencies and customers alike are trying to 'get digital'. Online marketing has the scope to deliver truly innovative campaigns that are individually targeted and add value to any brand. As the industry evolves and delivers superior results more and more money is moved away from traditional advertising to online.

With 10 years experience, Imano have been at the forefront of online marketing working with a range of companies from successful ecommerce companies to global airlines. We wanted to provide a structured resource that encapsulated our knowledge and experience whilst providing a simple guide that will help both the novice and experienced online marketer. We have left the intricacies of branding and CRM to other books that can deliver on the subject better. We know that online marketing is a fast changing field and that this book may soon be out of date but until then it remains our best resource.

Due to the nature of online marketing, some of the marketing options like organic search engine optimization are technically challenging whilst email marketing will feel familiar to the traditional direct marketer. We have looked at media planning, pay per click and organic search engine optimization, email marketing, affiliate marketing, viral marketing, Rich Media advertising and social marketing. We have also dedicated a chapter to analytics which is the measurement and analysis of online marketing activity.

The future of marketing may be all turning online from electronic billboards to digital paper and with IPTV (TV through broadband connections on phone lines) already here the platform for the future of online marketing is already apparent.

Online Media Planning

Media planning forms the basis of any online marketing activity and allows you to build campaigns to reach your target audience and measure results against your objectives. The greatest benefit of using online media is the ability to track and quantify campaigns (see the analytics chapter), especially when conducting brand building exercises. This advanced tracking enables you to target campaigns to deliver the best Return on Investment (ROI) and this capability has helped the online industry grow by 60%[2] in 2004. In the same period, total advertising expenditure grew by only 5.8%[3]. Online media expenditure is growing more rapidly than conventional media such as radio, TV, direct mail & outdoor. The fundamental reason for the growth is down to the effectiveness and accountability of the medium.

Media planning for online requires knowledge of each of the different media formats involved, including organic search, pay per click, viral, affiliate, Rich Media, email, viral and social marketing (blogs, vBlogs, Podcasting, RSS).

Online media planning follows a process from beginning to end:
- **Campaign research** – Identify the campaign objectives, target audience, competitive intelligence, audience reach and campaign/budget testing.

- **Creating the media plan** – Selecting the relevant online media properties, portals, search engines, online publishers or email lists.
- **Media buying** – Negotiating contracts and delivering the media.
- **Analyze and evaluate the plan** – Monitor Key Performance Indicators (KPI) in real time and evaluate the execution of the plan.

In the following sections, we will cover these in detail.

Campaign Research

Step 1 – Identify your campaign objectives

The first step is to identify your campaign objective, which can be either:

Direct Response – The campaign objective is to get the customer to make a 'call to action' so either a purchasing decision or request for more information. An example of a direct response campaign could be a low cost airline sending out an email with the objective to get an immediate response for the consumer to book a cheap flight offer.

Brand Building – The campaign objective is to raise awareness about a brand. In this case, an example would be a banner emphasizing that an airline has more leg room in relation to its competitors.

Step 2 – Identify your target audience

The next step is to define the target audience. This is dependant on the campaign objectives. A brand building exercise will typically cast a wide demographic net, for example a funky fashion retailer trying to raise awareness of their new product range will target all men and women aged between 18 and 35. Whereas a direct response campaign may be more selective to get the best targeted response, for instance if the same retailer was trying to promote their new low waist designer jeans for women they would target only female college students who come from an AB1 household aged between 18 and 21. There are a number of different ways in which you can define your target audience, and this is called your target demographic. Below we have identified a typical set of demographics that should be used when defining your target media consumers.

Demographic	Description	Example
Sex	Whether the target is male, female or either sex	Male
Age	The age group of the targeted audience	18-35
Earnings	The household earnings of the audience	$50K+
Job	The position held by the audience	Media planner
Ethnic Group	The race of the desired audience	Asian
Family Members	How many members in the family	Two Children
Marital Status	Whether the target is single, or married	Married
Geographic/Persona/Behavioral		
Geographic location	Target location of audience	London
Personas	Fictional people who are identified as the typical customer/user	Bob aged 20, living in Boston with a cat and enjoys swimming
Behavioral Targeting	The real time needs of the audience at the time of viewing the advert	Researching a holiday to Morocco

The information in the previous table makes it easier to select the correct online media for the specific campaign. There are industry extensions to demographic profiling. Standards available include; MOSAIC, an internationally recognized zip/postcode based system that can predict purchasing behavior not just by the area in which you live but even by the street, ACORN, a UK system based on census data and lifestyle information organized by postcode. Using these standard systems can be beneficial in matching your demographic with media owners/publishers, who also use standardized demographics to identify their users. Overall, this makes it easier to identify all media that matches your requirements.

Another approach to identifying and targeting your audience is through persona creation. A persona represents a typical person within your customer base. It is a notional, real human with a name, face, motivations, attitudes and goals. When developing your personas, you need to have a good understanding of the characteristics of your customers. The key questions to pose are:

- Who are your customers?
- What are their needs and goals?
- What are they doing and how are they doing it?
- What is the environment or context of their situation?

To create personas, use information compiled from demographic, psychographic and topographic data

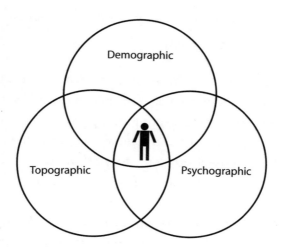

Demographic
Customer profile including; age, gender, ethnicity, income, martial status.

Psychographic
These are characteristics based on the consumers' ethics, values and psychological beliefs. What other factors does the customer consider during the buying process? This data may be revealed by research, for example, focus groups, interviews and blogs.

Topographic
A model that integrates demographic and psychographics with detailed buying process data , identifying clusters or patterns.   A

good topographic profile will give you a view on your customers' needs and motivations.

Using the profiles shown above you can create your personas. Start with a small set of possibly four personas and extend this out after testing. The key to creating strong personas is the use of a customer story. Each persona will have a personality and you should be able to pose a problem story followed by a solution. Personas can be applied to much of online marketing.

Behavioral targeting tends to ignore traditional demographic requirements, instead focus on the behavior of a user prior to viewing the advert. Behavioral media planning works on the principle of triggers and events and is a fairly new form that is unique to the online world. Organizations using this form of media planning often find much higher conversion rates. An example of behavioral targeting is:

Behavior or Trigger	Event
1. Customer logs on to a general portal between 6pm – 8pm 2. Then searches for local cinemas 3. Browses through results, but does not click to view movie details. 4. Clicks away from results to browse other pages	Show a Rich Media overlay which promotes a new TV show on the television at 8pm tonight.

Step 3 – Competitive intelligence

To be successful, you need to understand the performance of your competitors. The ability to use this information to your advantage based on their relative strengths and weaknesses is of key importance. There are a number of services available that log and store campaigns, from banner ads to emails sent. In addition, there are also tools from companies such as Hitwise[4] that are invaluable at providing detailed breakdown of site conversions, traffic, search click-through, pay per click keywords, sponsorship campaigns and affiliate traffic for all your competitors' sites.

Step 4 – Defining campaign reach

Campaign reach is the number of people that will be exposed to your campaign. In traditional media the metric used to be called Gross Rating Points (GRP). A GRP is calculated by multiplying reach (the number of people who will see your message) with frequency (the number times that person will see your message). The importance of reach varies by campaign type, it is more important when running a brand building campaign than in a direct response campaign. Campaign reach can normally be estimated for all online media including search and social marketing by using tools that provide analysis of the traffic for a site.

Step 5 – Setting the budget

Many campaigns are rolled out with a pre-defined budget however many organizations are willing to trial a campaign to gauge the ROI. Based on the performance, a company will decide on the budget to allocate. It is essential to define a budget prior to finalizing the plan.

Creating the Media Plan

Step 6 – The plan

There are number of different online advertising options which should be considered in the online media plan. The most commonly used formats are described in the following table.

Creative Format	Standard Billing Metric	Average Click-through Rates	Examples
Rich Media	CPM (Cost per Thousand Impressions)	4%	Overlay: An interactive flash animation that appears on top of a web page for 10 seconds.
Standard Banners	CPM	0.5%	468 x 60 Standard banners
Sponsorship	Tenancy	0.5%	Partnership agreement to appear on the shopping pages of an ISP
Pay per Click (PPC)	CPC (Cost per Click)	8%	Appearing on sponsored listings on search engines, including contextual advertising
Email Lists	CPM	5%	Renting a third party opt-in email list from a portal
Feed Advertising	CPC	0.5%	Creating an RSS feed/ Product feed that links to your site
Pay per Call	PPC (Pay per Call)	5%	Listing a telephone number on an advert and paying every time a user calls that number.

Online marketing is currently in a stage of rapid evolution and new marketing formats are available every month. New formats include Podcasting, RSS Feeds and Blogs, these offer great value during the start-up phase as costs are minimal and novelty factor is high. Although, when the format matures and a robust marketing model is created, prices rise and response rates will often fall.

After identifying all the media formats in the plan, the next step in the media planning process is to select the relevant media (see following chapters), these include:

- Internet sites
- Email lists
- Affiliate programs
- Blogs
- Podcasts
- Sponsorships
- Viral campaigns
- Search Engine Keywords

Once you have identified the relevant media that matches your target demographic and your advertising creative format you can role out a test campaign with the minimum budget, evaluate the results and roll out the full budget on the best performing media.

A/B testing allows you to identify the best advertising creative and the best media properties. It is a simple process of running the same advert on many sites to find the best performing sites or alternatively running different adverts on the same site to find the best performing advertising.

It is important to remember that a media plan is more than just selecting the relevant sites, email lists, keywords or viral campaign - the plan should also specify details of the campaign including:

- Exact pages on the site
- Time and dates you want the media to display
- Duration of the campaign
- Position of the advert on the page
- How long the advert will appear on the page
- What interactions will take place
- Number of times the advert will be shown to the same user
- Advert size
- Keywords
- Viral competition or game

- Affiliate commission structure
- Prizes
- Any behavioral targeting

The final plan should include the following for each separate media buy:

- Type of media
- Name of media owner/site/email list
- Total exposure on media
- Estimated total costs
- Estimated response rate/success rate
- Specifics of delivery
- Estimated ROI

Media Buying

Step 7 - Negotiating the deal

When buying your search pay per click or affiliate marketing there is little room for negotiation but with much of the other media there can be. Part of the media buying process is one of validating all the figures in the plan and where possible negotiating the terms as listed in the media plan. Organizations may want to use Request for Proposals (RFP's) to ask for the best rates for running a campaign from a media owner. A rate card is a standard price offered to all advertisers and is available from all serious media publishers. When negotiating, media buyers should try establishing preferred rates either for longer term deals, pre-negotiated contracts or bulk buys across a range of media properties owned by a single publisher or represented by a single network.

There are three different ways in which banner advertising media can be bought:

- **Specific booking** – this is when the advertiser has specifically asked for that media.
- **Network buys** – this is when the advertiser has defined some form of targeting but has not defined the media.
- **Blind buys** – this is when the advertiser has only specified the media format and has very little control on where the advert is displayed.

A key note here is that the more specific a media buyer, the higher the cost.

Step 8 - Delivering the media

This is often the easiest step in the whole process: it varies from media to media, and includes setting up your search keywords, establishing your affiliate program, delivering your email or making your viral or advertising campaign live. For banner or Rich Media campaigns there are a number of advert delivery companies who are already pre-integrated on to the publisher's site to deliver a range of media formats and there is usually more than one per publisher. Unless you are using an agency that is managing the whole process for you, it's normally the buyer's role to manage the delivery of the media and to keep track of the complete processes to ensure that campaigns are completely delivered and any discrepancies need to be identified immediately.

Monitoring and Evaluating the Campaign

Step 9 - Tracking and analyzing the campaign

As we mentioned earlier, the key component of online marketing is that the budget is accountable because you can track everything from click-though to sale. Therefore, organizations know exactly what they are getting for each dollar they spend, unlike media like radio and TV where this can only be a prediction. When running an online media campaign, organizations should make sure the following forms of tracking are in place to be able to analyze the campaign in detail:

- Track every link on the campaign.
- Track every delivery of the campaign.
- Using cookies to track a user's activities after viewing the campaign (usually for a period of 30 days).
- Track all sales from a campaign.

- Monitor overall activity prior, during and after a campaign.
- For search campaigns, track the performance by keyword.
- For affiliates, track your best performing affiliates.
- For viral campaign, track the spread to people over time.

Further details on tracking and analyzing campaigns are described in the analytics chapter later in this book.

Step 10 - Evaluating the plan

Once the campaign has been delivered and all the results have been analyzed organizations need to look at how it compared against the objectives defined at the start. It is possible that your campaign will not develop exactly as expected. This step will not only enable you to evaluate your plan but also make improvements on future campaigns so that the targets set from the beginning are closer to the actual results at the end of the campaign.

Tips

1. Run A/B testing to find the best adverts and the best media sites.

2. Look at ROI and not costs of the media, as Rich Media creative almost always provide 10-20 times higher click-through rates than standard banners but only cost 3-5 times as much.

3. Keep a good eye on the delivery of your advertising to

ensure that the media owner will fulfill their side of the agreement.

4. Use your own analytics to manage any discrepancies.

5. Use behavioral targeting to improve conversion rates.

Search Engine Pay Per Click Advertising

Search Engine Pay Per Click Advertising

Search engine advertising, often referred to as Pay per click (PPC) advertising has seen a phenomenal growth rate with Forrester estimating that expenditure in Europe alone is set to reach $3.5 billion by 2010.[5] Its success has been in its simplicity at delivering qualified traffic to a site. A typical PPC advertisement consists only of text which is split into a short title and slightly longer description. These adverts appear at various places on the page when a user types in relevant keywords into a search engine and are often displayed with the title 'sponsored links'. The major search engines like Google, Yahoo and MSN have their own PPC program, whilst smaller search engines tend to have relationships with the larger search companies PPC programs.

Definition of Goals

Before the start of a campaign it is essential to define its goal. This goal could be site exposure, traffic, email registrations, bookings, orders, revenue or a combination of these. With these goals in mind it becomes easier to measure performance and extrapolate daily figures to ensure that you are on target to reaching your desired return on investment (ROI).

Designing for Personas

Looking at personas is an important part of creating your campaign. A persona illustrates a typical person within each of your customer segments. For a typical cosmetics site, one persona could be, Jill 24, web designer, single who is looking for big branded makeup, another could be Mary 46, housewife, mother of two looking for anti-aging products. With all of these personas in mind it becomes easier to create adverts that are targeted and will be more compelling to a particular persona.

Stage in Buying Process

Depending on the type of product you sell there are a number of stages that a consumer will go through to make a purchasing decision. For example, the amount of research done on a car before purchase is different to branded cosmetics purchases. Consequently, it is important to create adverts that are orientated to the customer's stage in the buying process. A discount or buy now to save 50% will be a much more effective campaign if the consumer is in the final stages of purchasing, whilst an early stage product researcher is going to be more interested in objective reviews or ratings.

Geo-targeting

You can target your PPC adverts by country based on the geographical regions your site operates. You should localize your adverts as much as possible and track the results from each regional campaign.

Age, Gender Targeting

The latest PPC engines, in particular MSN, also allow targeting by age and gender. This enables you to target each advert based on your target persona.

Keyword Selection

Keyword analysis is an important element of any PPC activity and focuses on creating a list of the most relevant keywords to bid on. Each PPC engine has keyword selection tools that help you identify keywords and keyword combinations to bid on. These tools also give you an estimation of traffic for particular keywords. Using your site conversion data and these traffic figures you can get a prediction on the sales you will generate. There is considerable competition on popular keywords and therefore a higher cost per click, so it is important to select the broadest list of keywords to ensure that you have a lowest average cost per click. Each of the PPC engines has its own nuances and provides options to ensure either exact matches of bidding terms or partial matches on searched keywords. Make sure that all the keywords options are considered as things like broad matching on keywords like 'flight' would make your advert appear every time 'flight' was searched in any keyword combination. For instance, even searches for 'flight arrivals information' would bring up your advert whilst searches for 'flight Dubai' may be relevant you would end up paying a higher bid cost than bidding directly for the keyword combination 'flight Dubai'. In addition, to the keywords you bid on you can also set up negative keywords for which you would like your adverts to not appear for, making sure that you increase your relevancy. For instance, you could have added 'arrivals' as a negative keyword to ensure that your advert did not appear for 'flight arrivals information'.

Compelling Advert Copy

A PPC advert is most likely to get clicked on if it clearly matches with the keywords that the user searched on. If for example a user searches on 'Cheap Sony TVs' and your advert had the title 'Cheap Sony TVs' and the description 'Buy Cheap Sony TVs at the lowest prices - Buy today and get free delivery' then this would certainly match the search and would get a high click-through rate. The problem with this is that on PPC adverts you only pay if the person clicks the advert, so to maximize your budget you would need to pre-qualify clicks to know whether the potential customer was really interested in what you advertised. This is often done by adding prices and clarifying the advertisement. For example, the above Sony advert may change to 'Buy Cheap Sony TVs' with the full text to 'Buy Cheap Sony TVs from only $150 for a 21" widescreen.' This advert would get fewer clicks as people would only click on it if they were prepared to pay $150 for the lowest end TV. This would ensure that only serious shoppers clicked and therefore increase your post-click conversion and ROI. Most adverts can easily be optimized through a process of A/B testing where different adverts are created and tested against each other to see which one performs the best. This process is repeated to make sure that the adverts are as effective as possible.

Landing Page

After someone clicks an advert it should take them to a page that clearly reflects the content of the advert they selected. For example, a 'Sony TV Ad' should click-through to a page that clearly displays the different range of Sony TVs and their prices with strong buying incentives like 'Free Shipping'. PPC adverts often link to a product page from a PPC advert but this page may not be as effective as a specially created landing page. This is often due to compromises in layout and design to either make product pages more search engine friendly or limitations with ecommerce systems, whereas a landing page can be completely customized to convert customers with a more compelling magazine style layout. A specially designed landing page creates a much better conversion than forcing someone to a home page and then making them search for the products on the site again with the obvious risk of them giving up. It is also important that similar to PPC adverts landing pages should be tested through A/B testing to ensure that they are as effective as possible.

Optimization

A/B Testing or multi-variant testing is currently the best way of optimizing a campaign. Here multiple versions of the campaign are run. Each time a single variable is changed to see which campaign works the best. The more favorable campaign is kept and then another variable changed. The variables could be anything from advertising copy to a bid amount.

Contextual Advertising

PPC click adverts can be delivered on sites other than the search engine itself. These adverts appear on web pages and are automatically selected to best reflect the content of the page where they are run. These contextual adverts have been a boon for developers of smaller web sites and have generated considerable amounts of revenue for them and PPC search engine programs. When setting up adverts on PPC engines there are normally options to enable your adverts to appear on other sites (contextually) or not. Depending on the kind of adverts you have and where they run, it may or may not be effective, so it is essential to track contextual advertising separately.

Bidding Tools

A number of bidding tools are available that let you manage keywords across multiple PPC providers as well as implement more advanced bidding strategies like timed bids. These tools can integrate to the site and make it easier to base your bidding on set ROI or a specific cost per sale.

Bidding Strategies

Advertisers should focus on a strategy that meets with their goal. Often bidding becomes a game based on averages and therefore some keywords are overbid to reach an overall target. For example, a company could set a target of 1,000 orders but it may be easier to sell an inexpensive low value item compared to higher margin items, as a result bids would increase on the low value item to improve the average. This is the main reason that goals need to be clearly defined. There needs to be more than a set revenue or number of orders/bookings but rather a more comprehensive ROI strategy based on profit.

CPA/CPC/Conversion

The CPA/CPC/Conversion matrix can give you an idea of the amount that you can bid for keywords, at varying CPC and conversion rates. Using this matrix you can see that an increase in bid amount cannot give you a lower CPA without any changes in conversion, so remember that if your ad doesn't work at the current bid amount increasing it is unlikely to help.

Cost Per Acquisition (CPA) by CPC and Conversion

	Cost per Click (CPC)				
Site Conversion	$0.10	$0.15	$0.20	$0.25	$0.30
1%	$10.00	$15.00	$20.00	$25.00	$30.00
2%	$5.00	$7.50	$10.00	$12.50	$15.00
3%	$3.33	$5.00	$6.67	$8.33	$10.00
4%	$2.50	$3.75	$5.00	$6.25	$7.50
5%	$2.00	$3.00	$4.00	$5.00	$6.00

API Integration

The major PPC engines have an Application Programming Interface (API) that enables your systems to directly use the PPC systems. You can normally create new adverts, check keywords, change bids or report on click-throughs. For instance, API integration into your ecommerce system could allow you to disable an advert when stock levels are depleted. It could also be as clever as knowing that someone is about to complete an order for the last stock of an item and switch off adverts to stop traffic in advance of stock running out. Management of bid campaigns can become very time consuming so API integration can take some of the work out of running multiple campaigns across multiple PPC companies, and can allow easier A/B testing to perform continuous campaign optimization.

Three Major Programs

Google AdWords

Run by Google, advert positions are based on bid amount and click-through rate. It is not immediately obvious how much other people are bidding to appear in their current position. Certain adverts that appear higher on the listings may be paying less per click as their advert has a higher click-through rate either because it is better designed or is more relevant to the search keywords.

Yahoo Search (formerly Overture)

Overture was purchased by Yahoo and renamed. Currently, ad positions are based on bid amounts only so it is clear who is paying what for each position. This may change in the future.

MSN Search

The latest entry into the PPC market with adverts appearing on MSN, the advert positions are based on a bid amount and click-through rate similar to Google.

Click Fraud

A strongly debated topic is click fraud. Click fraud occurs when a PPC advert is clicked by either a human or computer that has no interest in the advert but only clicks it to cost the advertiser additional money or generate money for themselves. All the major PPC providers try hard to use technology to combat this, though it is often difficult for them to unearth lower volume fraudulent clicks particularly from competitors and especially if they are coming from various IP addresses. It is important that as an advertiser you have your own set of tools for measuring advertising performance in addition to the ones supplied by the PPC engines. This way any discrepancies can easily be identified and reported back to the search engines for investigation.

Search Engine Optimization

Search Engine Optimization

After a user searches on a set of keywords on Google they are presented with a page of search results composed of sponsored listings (covered in the previous chapter) and in the main section of the page, the organic listings. Organic search engine optimization (SEO) is about increasing the number of visitors that your site gets from a search engine. This is achieved by getting more documents indexed on the search engine and by attaining a higher position in the results. The problem for many marketers and traditional advertising agencies lies in the technical nature of search engines and the difficulty in understanding the underlying algorithms that produce the rankings for particular keyword searches.

Search engines are split into directories that use manual submission and people to build their directories and the indexers that search throughout the net for content using electronic robots named bots or spiders. Due to the vast and continued growth of the internet, indexer search engines have taken precedence with some search engines like Yahoo providing a mix of results from both its directory and indexes. As the vast majority of web sessions, 88%[6] start at a search engine this has become a major focus for marketers.

The most popular search engine is Google which accounts for

the greatest number of search requests[7] and this is the search engine that we have focused on when delivering the content for this chapter. This is not to say that other search engines are not important or that they use the same algorithm but that Google's success has ensured that many search engines are moving in the same direction and since Google have filed their search patent[8] we do not have to rely on the typical conjecture in this field. Importantly, Google ensures that there is a level of feedback from users through the Google toolbar that enables Google to refine their search results over time. Also, a significant part of Google's algorithm is to protect its search engine against search SPAM which is the use of techniques to improve a site's rankings normally through the artificial creation of links, so we have outlined the main areas to watch out for.

We suggest an approach that focuses on continuous improvement in a structured way rather than anything that the search engines could interpret as trying to manipulate the results. We believe that the best way to reach the top spots is to align with the search engines' goal which is to deliver the best and most relevant results for their users, we call it 'alignment' strategy. This will ensure that you consistently rank highest amongst your competitors and do not get black-listed. In the following sections, we are going to clarify the elements that are analyzed by Google. Using this information it starts to become clear what is needed for organic search engine success.

Document Inception Date

The document inception date is the date the document was created, first indexed or linked to or the first registration date of the domain. The inception date is used to determine the rate of growth of links to a document. For example, a document with yesterday's inception date with 10 links to it could be scored higher than a document with an inception date of 10 years ago and a 100 links to it. For some searches that are made on a search engine, an older document may be more favorable than a newer document therefore older documents may be ranked higher and vice-versa.

SPAM Check

Chart the link growth to see if there is a natural growth. A spiky growth could indicate SPAM.

Rate of link growth

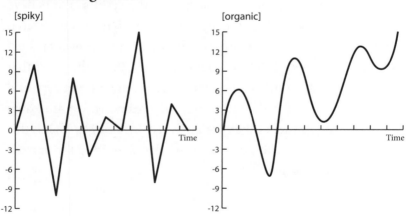

Tip

Have a structured link building program & don't buy links or try to SPAM the search engine.

Content Updates/Changes

Every document has parts that are more important to the search engine like the main piece of content on the page and elements that are much less important like JavaScript code, date/time information, adverts or boiler plate information. Using the relative importance of each element the search engine looks at the frequency and amount of changes over time. For example, changes to the content would have significantly more importance than changes to advertisements on a site. Google looks at whether fresher or staler documents are preferred by a search user and then ranks fresher or staler documents higher, accordingly. For example, people searching for 'Top of the league' would prefer a fresher document than perhaps people that were searching for information on 'Winner of 1982 World Cup'

Tip

Look at whether Google favors fresh or stale documents by conducting a search and seeing if the top results are from fresher or staler documents. Once you have this information you will have an idea of how often or not to update the main content elements of your document.

Query Analysis

Google analyses the volume and kind of searches that users make through the search engine. It analyses these results over time and documents associated with the fastest growing keyword searches are ranked higher as they could indicate a hot topic or breaking news story. Google also looks at search terms and records whether a search term should produce a consistent set of results or whether searches like 'World Cup Winning Team' should produce a different set of results every year.

SPAM Check

If a document appears highly in the search results for a discordant set of search results, then it may be considered as SPAM and ranked lower as it is unlikely for one document to be a good source for a number of different topics.

Tip

Each document should be optimized and contain information related to a few searched for keywords. If you try and put all the keywords into one document then you are unlikely to rank very highly and are much more likely to be considered as search engine SPAM.

Link Based Criteria

Google looks at the number of links to a document (back links) and the growth or disappearance of these links over time. A downward trend in the number of links to a document, decline in the rate of link growth or disappearance of links may indicate that a document is getting stale whilst an upward trend in links and rate of link growth may indicate that a document is fresh. In addition, detailed graphs of link growth over time can be used to show particular patterns for fresh documents, stale documents, those that may no longer be updated or that have been superseded. Also, a weight may be given to every link based on the freshness of the overall document in which it is contained. Links from authoritative sources, like Government pages are weighted higher.[9]

SPAM Check

The dates that links appear can be used to detect if links are SPAM. A 'legitimate' document attracts back links slowly whilst a sudden growth in links particularly from documents without editorial discretion, like guest books, referrer logs, 'free for all' pages could indicate SPAM.

Tip

Make sure that you have a link building program in place that lets you grow your links organically by:

1. Asking suppliers, customers and partners to link to you.
2. Submitting to online discussion forums.
3. Creating a blog.

4. Submitting to shopping portals and industry sites.

5. Offering something great like a free gift or service so other sites value linking to you.

6. Creating your own affiliate program where all the links are direct to you.

Remember, you can always analyze your competitors to see who links to them. You can then contact these sites to see if you can get the same links to you, too. Normally, you just type into a search engine 'link:Site URL' to get a list of the links, where Site URL is your competitor's full URL (e.g. www.competitiorwebsite.com).

Anchor Text

Anchor text is the clickable text that is associated with a link. Google looks at the anchor text, freshness of the anchor text and changes to the anchor text over time.

SPAM Check

If there is a disparity between the anchor text and the document that it links to, possibly due to changes in domain ownership, Google could look at the time this occurred and ignore all the valuable links to your document prior to this event.

Tip

Let people link to you with appropriate anchor text.

Traffic

Google will look at the traffic that a document gets and changes to that traffic over time. It will also consider seasonal, daily or other timely changes to see if a document receives more traffic at these times and is therefore more relevant at these times. Any significant drop in traffic may indicate that a document is stale. Google may also consider 'advertising traffic' separately.

Tip
The more relevant traffic you get the better.

User Behavior

Google analyses the amount of time that a user spends on a site after he/she has clicked a link from a search results page. If there is a significant decline in the time spent on the site then it could indicate that the document contains information that is out of date and has become stale. For instance, if after clicking from a Google search results link to a timetable, an average person spent 2 minutes on the site and now the average was under 30 seconds, it would indicate that the timetable was out of date. Google collects this information using the Google toolbar.

Tips
Make your site the ideal source for your product/service so people spend the longest time there. Any documents that have

become stale should easily link through to the fresher version e.g. a product that you no longer sell should link through to the replacement product.

Domain Related Information

Information that you used to register your domain name, including contact information, length of registration and nameservers (servers that resolve your domain name to IP address i.e. www. imano.com resolves to IP 213.52.208.230) is used to determine the legitimacy of domains. People that tend to deceive the search engines with SPAM doorway pages often only register domain names for the shortest period of time normally one year whilst legitimate domains are registered for considerably longer. Google uses pattern matching between information about your domain with that of known illegitimate domains. Google also looks at whether this contact information, hosting company or nameservers has changed relatively often.

SPAM Check

A good nameserver is likely to host domains from a variety of domains and to have a history of hosting those domains, whilst a bad nameserver may be hosting domains for pornography sites, doorway pages or domains with commercial words (common indicator of SPAM) or primarily bulk domains from a single registrar or the nameserver may be brand new. Brand new nameservers are not necessarily bad unless having a combination of other negative factors.

Tips

The cheapest domain registrar is likely to have registered a large number of doorway domains. Use someone reputable who registers domains for corporate companies.

- Find ISPs by doing a WHOIS lookup on highly ranked sites.
- Use nameservers from top level ISPs.
- Use a reputable corporate ISP who does not deal with pornography domains.
- Register your domain for as long as possible, ideally 10 years.

Ranking History

Google will look at the historical ranking of a document to help determine the current ranking. A historically highly ranked document will have an influence on the current ranking. A document that falls significantly in rank would be flagged as 'out of favor' and may be considered outdated.

SPAM Check

A document that jumps in ranking across a number of queries might be a topical document or could be SPAM. Commercial queries can be repeated and documents that are ranked highly can be flagged and checked for SPAM. The change in rank over time is considered to see if a document is SPAM. If there is a sudden spike and the document is not linked to or from an authoritative or trusted source, like a news article, then a document may be considered as SPAM.

Tip
Try to get links from trusted news and authoritative sites

User Maintained/Generated Data

Google looks at the number of people and the growth in people that add a document to their internet browser's bookmarks/favorites. The basis of this is that people would only add a site to their bookmark/favorites, if the site would be useful in the long term and wanted to visit the site in the future. Google looks at the number of people that then use these bookmarks/favorites to rank a document higher. Conversely, a decline in the number of bookmarks, their usage or deletion of bookmarks could indicate that a document is out-dated and no longer relevant. Google gathers this information from the users of the Google toolbar.

Tip
Add links on your site to encourage people to bookmark this site or add it to their favorites list.

Unique Words, Bigrams, Phrases in Anchor Text

Google analyses the unique words, bigrams (pairs of letters, words or syllables) and phrases in anchor text for a document.

SPAM Check

Google analyzes graphs of unique words, bigrams, and phrases in anchor text to see if this information is real. Results that are created artificially would show spiky graphs whilst natural data would show organic graphs.

Tip

Don't try and SPAM the search engine using unscrupulous link trading or search companies as you could get black-listed and not recover from a lowered ranking.

Linkage of Independent Peers

SPAM Check

A sudden increase in the number of sites that link to you or links from unrelated sites (independent peers) would indicate SPAM. Particularly, if the anchor text of the links are very similar or unusually different in an attempt to fool the search engine.

Document Topic

Google attempts to extract the topic of a document using the URL, low frequency words contained in the document, categorization, content analysis, clustering or summarization.

SPAM Check

If Google sees a significant change in the number of topics associated with a document after a stable period of set topics or the disappearance of the original topic, Google may consider that the document has been taken over as a 'doorway page' and may consider the document and any links or anchor text associated with the document as SPAM.

Tip

Ensure your site stays consistent with its original topic.

Localization

Pick regional search engines you want to appear on based upon the countries you trade in. If you sell to France and you want to appear on Google.fr, the French version of Google, you should either host your site in France or have a French domain that your site can be indexed under.

It is important to continue repeating these steps on a structured basis and planning in advance of seasonal trends like Holiday

Season. Over a period of time the keywords will change in relevancy as search terms evolve and the relevancy of your product range changes.

With an analytics system you should be able the see what words are working for you, the traffic they are bringing in and the level of conversion you are getting for them. With this information, you can see how much of an improvement you have made and also if any changes you have made have improved your results. You can read more about this in the analytics chapter of this book.

Tips

1. Good content is essential – make sure you are providing the perfect source for the search engine by using 'alignment' strategy.
2. Have a link building strategy that gets great sites to link to you.
3. It has never been more important to have a good hosting company and ISP for your site.
4. Never SPAM the search engine.
5. Success doesn't happen over-night.

Email Marketing

Email Marketing

With email now the preferred communication channel for many people, companies are finding it particularly effective for marketing communications with customers. In an attempt to build the allusive one-to-one relationship, every email can be personalized to include content for an individual. Emails can be simple plain text or include full graphics using html. Many of the concepts associated with email marketing originate from the direct marketing industry. Complexities with email providers checking for unsolicited email (SPAM) make email marketing a constantly evolving field. This improved SPAM checking technology is ensuring that consumers only receive the messages that they really want to, so it has become even more important for every campaign to be relevant and targeted. The following chapter draws together key information on growing your database and delivering effective email campaigns.

Growing Your Email List

After spending substantial amounts on marketing to get traffic to your site it is essential to try and get your potential customers' email addresses to ensure that even if they do not complete a purchase now, you can market them and sell them additional products or services later. This email address with site statistics can enable you to push special offers for the items that the customer looked at or added to their basket but did not complete an order for.

Many people will be reluctant to give you their email address for nothing, unless you are a very trusted brand, so incentivizing the collection of an email address will increase your email registrations. An appropriate incentive or aspirational prize can also help to qualify the registrants. See the following examples:

Company	Example of email registration incentive
Airline Network	Competition to win a pair of KLM return flights to a destination of your choice
BuyCosmetics.com	3 Months free magazine subscription
Burger King	Basketball shoot out game, register & play to get your name on the leader board
CNN	Member service/ restricted area for news content & news/sports alerts sent to your email
Diesel	'Join the Cult' - 5 star member service, information on pre-launch products, invitations to exclusive Diesel fashion shows & parties, limited edition catalogs
Maybelline (L'Oreal)	Competition to win the latest product XXL Intense (intense & sexy lash kit)
Siebel	White paper & reports, complimentary Gartner Report for 'Reaping Business Rewards from CRM'
Virgin Wines	Free wine tasting course

Data Collection

The ideal scenario is to collect the email address directly from your home page, this will ensure you have the highest number of email address collected. After the collection of the opt-in email address (often called permission marketing[10]) you can redirect to a secondary page and collect additional information like age, sex and postal address. The more information you demand in the first instance the less likely the consumer will be to complete all the fields. If you fail to get the balance right the consumer will either enter incorrect information to move quickly through the process or not bother to finish the process at all. At each point you ask for information, provide an incentive for the consumer.

In the Diesel registration example, you could 'join the cult' with an email address, however it was followed up with an email to the consumer explaining they would only get the five star experience (launch parties, fashion shows) once they have registered with full details, including, age, sex, home address, telephone number and the two Diesel stores most frequented.

Segmentation

Targeting your emails to groups of people can be achieved through segmentation. Often this segmentation can be as simple as creating an email for an airline that is segmented to show flight costs from people's local airport. Organizations can gather information to conduct segmentation of lists either through the initial sign-up request, surveys, polls, re-registration requests or online analytics. Detailed segmentation can considerably increase the performance of campaigns by focusing specific promotions to specific target segments. Segmentation can also be conducted on customers based on their purchasing i.e. whether they have bought before, bought many times or have never bought. Looking at customer segments with an analytics tool it is possible to see the most profitable segments and put more effort into acquiring and retaining customers within these groups. Too much segmentation can lead to complicated campaigns that become difficult to manage on an ongoing basis so it is important to identify the key attributes of your customers and create focused campaigns.

Persona Creation

Creating personas, as outlined in the online media planning section, is a matter of putting a face to a typical customer within your target segment. It helps the whole organization to visualize the typical person that will respond to a campaign. Personas can be great at moving from a company-led view of the products or services to a more effective customer-led view. Done correctly, it will lead to a strategic framework that can be applied to all cross channel marketing activity and benefit the overall company.

Key Performance Indicators

It is important to evaluate the success of your email marketing and how you performed against your target. You could look at the following key performance indicators (KPI's) before and after activity to tell if the program is working:

- Increased product/service sales
- Increased brand loyalty – open & click-through rates of emails
- Greater conversion rates - click to sale from newsletters
- Greater proportion of returning visitors
- Less home page abandonment

Getting in to the Inbox

Focusing on the email delivery pipeline is essential. The basic principle of successful email marketing doesn't work if the message sits in the junk folder or worse still gets deleted by the email provider before it reaches the consumer's account. The objectives an email campaign is to:

Objective	Strategy
Get into the inbox	SPAM scoring and Add to safe list
Get the email opened	Subject line A/B testing
Captivate the consumer	Strong creative, clear & attractive offering
Generate a positive call to action	Easy to locate and nothing distracts the consumer from taking that call to action. (additional tactic, time limited offer)

Email providers go to considerable effort to ensure that SPAM does not get through to their customers email accounts. Email providers use sophisticated pattern matching to look at typical real non-commercial person-to-person email communication compared to those that come from volume commercial senders. Words like 'free' and 'special offer' and even 'unsubscribe' can stick you straight into the junk email boxes and with ever improving SPAM filters for both personal and work email accounts the best way to ensure your customer receives their email is to be added to their safe list and/or address book. It is impossible to force someone to add you to their list however on the following page are some tips that could help you gently encourage them to do so.

Strategy	Communication message/approach
Automated help depending upon the email provider	Step by step guide to how to add your email sender address to their safe list based on their email provider i.e. Hotmail, Yahoo, Gmail etc. at the point when the consumer registers with you
Include 'add to safe list' on every email	Repeat the message & make it easy; it may be a case of third time lucky. All emails should be customized for the email provider and offer help at the bottom on how to add your domain to their safe list
Time critical	Free give-away for the first 1000 people to reply, 10% off thereafter…add us to your safe list to make sure you don't miss out on this offer!
Prize incentivized + time critical	Add us to your safe list and win - winner must respond within 24 hours to collect the prize
Information critical	Your order confirmation may not be able to get through unless you add us to your safe list

Subject Lines

After getting into the Inbox, subject lines are the next key area to pay attention to when trying to increase the effectiveness of your email program.

Tip	Subject line	Consideration
Subject lines should indicate what you are offering. Having exceptionally high open rates isn't any good if it doesn't relate to what the email will contain and doesn't result in a click-through	Delivery information for your order	This may get very high open rates as it is a personal message however when the consumer opens the email to find a loan offer or car insurance it will immediately turn the consumer off and potentially damage your brand.
Test what gets in to the Inbox, some days 'free' might work	'Free delivery' verses 'Delivery at no cost'	Traditionally 'new' and 'free' are the best selling words in the English dictionary however it is important to remember that SPAM filters score these words badly often putting your email in the junk mail folder.
The subject line can include personal information like the receiver's name or town	Jane, we have a special offer for you Great deal on flights from Aberdeen airport	Remember this is a good tactic every so often, if you use it all the time it becomes boring and predictable for the consumer

Tips

- Is the subject line compelling?
- Does it fit into the view panel (if you have a subject line more than 10 words long will the consumer be able to read all of it? What would you loose if they couldn't?).
- Does the subject line reflect what is in the email content/ copy & 'call to action'?
- Can I personalize the subject line in any way to increase open rates?

A/B Testing

A/B testing is a term commonly used by direct marketing companies. It involves creating two versions of an email campaign and then modifying one variable to see which one performs better. It is important to look at open rates, clicks and post-click actions. This process can by repeated to develop the best performing campaigns. In a typical campaign, different subject lines, layouts, email types (html vs. plain text), promotions, prices, incentives or 'call to action' buttons can be tested to see which is most effective. Testing a number of these simultaneously is often called multivariant testing.

Behavioral Targeting

Further targeting of email can be based upon triggers such as a response to an earlier campaign or sales patterns. These campaigns are particularly effective because they are triggered by an event or set of events and can include very specific offers based on the previous behavior of the individual who is going to receive it.

This can be as simple as you emailing to ask if they would like to order more of a product when they are about to run out, or more advanced like looking at previous purchases to match offers and products. Personalization increases sales, and offering consumers specific offers based upon their previous interaction with you, can be very rewarding. For example:

Scenario	Subject line/Content
CD company knows a customer likes U2 as they bought one of their previous albums	Sally, want to get the latest U2 album first?....reserve your copy now
A clothing company would know your size and that you liked a particular brand based on previous purchases	Fred, we have just ten 32" waist Diesel jeans left
You were interested in a product and added it to your basket but didn't complete order	Bob, prices just lowered on MP3 players
You responded to and ordered a $10 coin collection	Simon, get this exclusive $100 coin collection

Email Frequency

How often would you like to receive an opt-in email? This often depends on the content of the email and its purpose. People are more likely to want a news story email daily than would want to see special offers, unless their job was buying! The ideal scenario is to let consumers select their preferred frequency. Though, this could become a problem if you do not have enough content or capability to produce an email on a very high frequency. Generally, once a month is too infrequent and may leave the consumer wondering who you are and once a day is probably too much. Again, the important thing is to base frequency around the customer, who would probably prefer to receive a greater frequency of gift suggestion emails around the Holiday Season to correspond with their greater purchasing desires.

Rationalizing the Database

Finally, with email marketing there comes a time when you draw a line underneath activity. There is a general reluctance to do this partly because of the low cost to continue to market to the list and partly because of a reluctance to delete an opt-in registration just in case the consumer was on the verge of buying when you chose to remove them.

If you have emailed a consumer continuously for 2 years and they never open an email is that person really interested in what you have to say? Rationalizing your database, enables you to:

- Understand when a campaign is successful with realistic open rates & click-throughs.
- Reduce cost…why send one million emails when 25% of the audience are diverting you to their Deleted Items.
- Maintain your brand, if someone doesn't want to hear from you even when they have opted-in, they will consider your emails to be SPAM.

Affiliate Marketing

Affiliate Marketing

Affiliate marketing is when an ecommerce site (merchant), pays a finder's fee to individuals or other companies (affiliates) who have agreed to send customers to their site. The affiliates will be paid either a fixed amount or a percentage of the sale based on the structure of the agreement. There are three different types of agreement:

1. **Pay Per Click (PPC)** – The affiliate will be paid for each time they send a visitor to the merchant's site.
2. **Pay Per Registration (PPR)** – The affiliate will be paid for each visitor that registers their details on the merchant's site.
3. **Cost per acquisition (CPA)** – The affiliate will be paid when a visitor successfully makes a purchase on the merchant's site.

The reason many merchants run affiliate programs is because the affiliate is only paid for results. Consequently, there is always a direct relationship between the revenue made by the merchant and the amount paid to the affiliates.

Creating the right affiliate program requires the following:

- Deciding on an in-house system or an affiliate provider
- Creating the program terms

- Designing adverts (banners, text links, emails, product feeds)
- Recruiting affiliates
- Monitoring performance
- Managing relationships
- On-going program and advertising updates

Earnings Per Click

The most important metric in running a successful affiliate program is Earnings per 100 clicks (EPC). EPC defines the earnings an affiliate will receive for every 100 clicks they send to the merchant. Logic dictates that affiliates will focus their attentions on merchants that provide the highest earnings For that reason, to run a successful affiliate program you will need to get to the top of the EPC chart for your sector. The top earning merchants can receive up to 50% of their total sales from affiliates.

In-house or Network

There are disadvantages and advantages to both. In the following table, we have created a cross comparison chart to help you decide which type of program is best suited for your business.

	Local Affiliate Network	**International Affiliate Network**	**In-house program**
Benefits	Small targeted network of affiliates All affiliates are in the same country Lower running costs Low technology investment and integration is simple	Manage your international activities through a single tool Very large pool of disparate affiliates Low technology investment	No override fee Links are direct to your site helping search engine ranking Higher level of customization
Disadvantages	No international coverage Still need to pay up to 30% as an override fee Links run through affiliate network	Complicated integration to manage multi – currency Still need to pay up to 30% as an override fee	Need to build or integrate affiliate technology Need to promote your own program to attract affiliates
Ideal for	Organizations which operate in one country only, and have a low budget assigned to technology and marketing a program	Organizations which operate in multiple countries, and have a greater technical capability but still have a limited affiliate program budget	Organizations with a strong brand who already have good flow of traffic to their site and have a healthy budget for technology and marketing the program

Creating the Program Terms

Regardless of the type of affiliate program you are running, organizations should standardize their program terms. There are a number of parameters which need to be considered:

- **Legal parameters** - contract duration and minimum commitments
- **Financial parameters** - such as when the affiliate is paid and how
- **Dispute resolution** - who has a final decision on affiliate payments
- **Commission structure** – percentages and breakpoints

If you are planning on using an affiliate network the program terms are already formulated and you will be guided through a wizard to customize components for your specific program. If you are creating your own affiliate program you should get your terms formed by a lawyer.

Commission Structure

The most important factor in creating your program terms and one of the main factors in the success of your affiliate program will be how you structure your commissions. In the table on the following page, we have highlighted the options available and provided guidelines to make your program successful.

Terms	Options	Guidelines
Type of payment	Pay a fixed fee per lead Pay a fixed fee per sale Pay a percentage of the sale Pay a commission every time the customer makes a sale	Paying a fixed fee works well if you are selling one or two products with similar profit margins. Paying a percentage of the sale is more workable with a large product range with varying price points. Commissions during the customer lifetime are only used when there are more merchants than first-rate affiliates.
Payment (only valid for fixed payment programs)	Pay a fixed payment per lead Pay a fixed payment per sale	The best affiliate schemes pay a fixed payment between $10 and $30 per lead/sale. This is only feasible if your CPA (Cost Per Acquisition) is within that limit. If not consider using a commission based payment. The more you can pay the better. The general rule is 30% of your net profit.

Terms	Options	Guidelines
Commissions (only valid for commission based programs)	Pay a commission on every sale Pay ongoing commissions during the customer lifetime	Commission based schemes are ideal when there is a large variation in your product prices, or your product value is low. The best schemes offer affiliate percentages of around 10% but this is dependant on industry and your margin, on commission schemes the general rule is 50% of your net profit.
Bonus payments	Single fixed bonus at set milestones Sliding commission scheme	In order to encourage your existing affiliates and to entice the larger affiliates, merchants need to offer great bonus schemes. A example would be: Payments of $1-$1,000 – 10% bonus Payments of $1,000-$5,000 – 15% bonus Payments of $5,000+ – 20% + $1,000 bonus

Affiliate Advertising

There are 3 different types of advertising options to consider when managing an affiliate program.

1. **Standard banners and emails** – These are industry sizes for banners for affiliates to place on their site and email templates which can be used by affiliates to send to their own lists.

2. **Product feeds** – A product feed is either an XML or CSV file of all your products with prices and links to your product. Affiliates can use this to create a product catalogue on their own sites.

3. **Text links** – This is a text based link that goes to your site. Affiliates can use this to add text links to their site or to run their own search engine pay-per-click program using these links.

Your affiliate program is competing with other programs for the affiliate's resources and your banners are competing with other content for attention so your advertising creative needs have to be perfect to get the best results. The more options you offer in terms of advert design and advert sizes the better. Affiliates can then select the ones most appropriate in relation to the other content on their site. It is also vital to keep your adverts up to date; an out-of-date advert could promote a sale that has already finished or an item you no longer stock, possibly boosting your clicks but at a low conversion rate which adversely affects your

EPC. An additional opportunity is to create landing pages for your top performing affiliates, as the click-through from the advert to the landing page will help conversion rates, in turn boosting your EPC.

Recruiting Affiliates

As well as keeping your EPC high, marketing your program to potential affiliates can bring in great rewards. Whether you are using an affiliate network or you have built an in-house system you need to spend time on the advertising creative and the copy. Once you have your program up and running you will need to do the following to market your program:

- Create a web based presentation to highlight your program include unique selling points (USPs) and display the basics of the program terms.

- Send an email to all potential affiliates. If you are running an in-house program you will be able to rent a list.

- Get actively involved in externally marketing the program. For example, participate in online affiliate forums to promote your program, consider running advertising in industry publications, or hold events.

Once the recruitment process is in place, the focus is on keeping affiliates. Affiliate retention strategies include:

- Creating a weekly affiliate's newsletter which keeps affiliates informed on promotions.

- Informing affiliates on best practices to achieve the greatest sales.
- Working with key affiliates to create customized advertising, or landing pages.
- Holding events for your top affiliates to better understand your brand and strengthen relationships.

Monitor Performance

Analytics is at the core of many marketing activities and affiliate marketing is no exception. Merchants need to track and analyze their program so they are able to understand what works and where improvement is needed. Metrics that are relevant include:

- EPC – keeping track on the EPC is vital. Merchants need to compare their EPC with others in the same sector.
- Sales metrics – tracking the number of orders, average order values, conversion rates per an affiliate.
- Advertising metrics – track the performance of each individual advert.

If you are using a network to manage your affiliate scheme, all the metrics will already be available. Metrics should then be used to improve your EPC, as follows:

- Inform affiliates of the best performing adverts; pass this information back to the design team so they know what works.
- Use benchmarking to see which affiliates are performing

well and market other affiliates with these best practices.

- Look at the advertising, affiliates and program terms of merchants with a successful EPC and use this intelligence for your program.

Tips

1. Spend time on your affiliate program; either have a full time person or hire an agency.
2. Keep all your banners up to date.
3. Keep track on your EPC. This is important. A good EPC will help attract the best affiliates.
4. Ensure any affiliates bidding on the same keywords are not driving up advertising cost.
5. Create landing pages for your best affiliates.

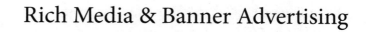

Rich Media & Banner Advertising

Rich Media & Banner Advertising

We've all seen thousands of banner adverts on the internet but can you remember the last one? Maybe, you can remember your favorite one that had a golf game in it but do you remember what brand it was for? Banner advertising is one of the earliest forms of advertising on the internet, so called because the adverts typically represented graphical banners across the page. The sizes were defined by the Interactive Advertising Bureau (IAB)[11] to commoditize the online advertising industry, taking adverts into a fixed set of sizes and styles similar to the 15 and 30 second ad slots on TV or 48 sheet posters. This makes it easier for sites to sell advertising and for advertisers to book using a clear set of sizes. Cost per Thousand impressions (CPM) is the normal unit of sales and is a cost for a thousand of the banner impressions to appear on a site, normally restricted to one per page. A few problems lay with the online formats, namely:

- The various computer screen sizes and resolutions people use make one size banner appear at various different sizes and take up a different proportion of the screen for people with different screen resolutions. You can't really imagine an advertiser in magazine being too happy about his full page advert appearing at smaller sizes in some magazines.

- The per impression billing model implies that an impression is where one person had seen that banner, where in reality it is quite possible for that banner to appear off the screen for some users because of screen resolution or browser window size.

- A longer term problem was the increased occurrence of banners which causes banner blindness where your brain just switches off to a particular size of picture because it knows it is an advert.

As online advertising has evolved so have the formats, we now have newer Rich Media formats so called because they offer a richer user experience. These formats are similar to TV adverts and often have an interactive element that lets users interact with the advert. This could be as simple as opening a box to reveal a product or more complicated implementations where you can check if flights are available directly on the banner. Forrester research predicts that Rich Media will start to take precedence over search in 2007[12]. These Rich Media banners are the other end of the online marketing spectrum from the simple pay per click text adverts and offer an ability to send a compelling message and allow a level of interaction that just wasn't available in any previous medium. The real key is to maximize on the potential to create truly branded experiences that leave the customer with a positive feeling.

Rich Media and Banner Formats

There are a number of popular formats that companies are working with:

1. **Video banners** – more and more people have broadband and running videos within banners is great for running

movie trailers or re-using TV advertising.

2. **Overlays** – run transparently on top of content pages.

3. **Expandables** – a simple banner that expands out when the user brings their mouse cursor over it.

4. **Interstitials** – full page advertising that displays before the content of a page loads.

5. **Transaction banners** – allowing full booking, flight check, ecommerce transactions straight from the banner.

6. **Dynamically generated** – where the banner loads frequently changing data like interest rates for a bank or betting odds.

7. **Interactive** – allowing interaction with the advert to experience the brand.

Interaction

The key advantage of online is the ability to interact with a campaign. A customer can not only see a campaign for a product but can also experience the product or brand values through interaction. This could take the form of dragging around an object, peeling or popping open a box to reveal a product to more complex actions that work as simple games. Marketing through experience is particularly valuable as it increases brand recall and can have a positive impact on the perception of a brand. Interaction has been so successful that many outdoor campaigns are starting to take this up with posters that contain touch-sensitive video screens.

Targeting

Successful targeting of campaigns can have exceptional results. For example, an airline banner on a travel destination site. The idea is to match the audience for your offering with the audience of the site running your campaign. This can be further advanced with detailed data that site owners have that lets them match campaigns to specific users (see Online Media Planning chapter). Also, the impact of Rich Media campaigns is ideal for behavioral targeting where a particular campaign is displayed based on specific triggers like a consumer clicking a combination of links.

Shows Per Session

Due to the higher impact of Rich Media campaigns you should make sure that a user does not get overwhelmed with your advert as a result, you probably want to restrict impressions to once per site visit.

Performance Measurement

Online marketing has the advantage that it can be measured in considerably more detail than traditional kinds of marketing. In particular, the level of clicks, interactions, or even the people that may have seen a campaign and then respond later. Three of the primary measurements are:

Post click event

This counts the people that click a banner and then those that either book, sign-up or buy from a site.

Post interaction event

This counts the number of people that interact with a banner but don't necessarily click-through to the site and later conduct a booking, sign-up or buy from the site. This is a good metric but doesn't consider that a user could have interacted with a banner by accident to reach the close button.

Post impression event

This counts the number of people that see a banner and then visit the site later and conduct a booking, signup or buy from the site. The main issue with this is that someone who sees a banner isn't necessarily influenced by the banner. This is particularly the case when it is applied to low impact 468 banners but less so to higher impact full page overlays.

The tools required to measure these figures often rely on technology like cookies, which some people disable and delete or JavaScript, which some people disable. Therefore, these metrics can only be best guesses and allowances need to made for measurement inaccuracy. It is important to have a single analytics system to ensure that impressions and revenue are not counted twice allocated across multiple sources.(see chapter on Analytics)

Viral Marketing

Viral Marketing

Viral marketing is often regarded as the allusive campaign that reaches more people by word of mouth than it ever reached in the original marketing activity. Viral marketing gains momentum by being shared between friends, family and co-workers. This has occasionally been achieved through traditional advertising like TV commercials that excite the target audience so much so that they are talked about everywhere. With the advent of the internet there is even more opportunity to create a viral marketing campaign by allowing the delivery of these campaigns on-demand through web sites, emails and applications.

Viral marketing has been a tough nut to crack for advertisers as often typical campaigns do not lend themselves to be shared with friends, but more and more companies are working around this by taking the experience of the product/service they sell and encapsulating that into an interactive piece of marketing that lets consumers take away the brand experience. Successful campaigns rely on more than simply forwarding attachments to friends and have fully interactive micro-sites. When viral marketing is done well it can produce exceptional results. In just one week at the end of October 2005, three of the fastest growing site audiences were due to viral campaigns led by Coors Beer with a 285 per cent increase in traffic.[13]

So how do you do it effectively? How will it help the brand and, most importantly, will it show up on the bottom line? Here are eight simple pointers and tips to ensure your viral campaign is effective.

1. Make it Simple to Interact

Decide what form a viral campaign should take: survey or questionnaire; competition or promotion with an incentive; humorous creative execution; or an interactive game or test. The form your campaign takes is important but remember no one has time to read pages of instructions and look at huge sections of terms and conditions before they get started. Let's make it easy and fun for them. If it is a game or quiz, make it completely obvious 'how to play'; we're all rushed for time, so make it simple.

Tip
Can you explain your campaign within 10 seconds?

2. Make it Relevant

To optimize message spread, content must be entertaining and engaging. You have to appeal to the vast majority of people to make a successful viral campaign. By definition the more people that it appeals to, the further it is likely to spread.

The success of a self-propelling, viral marketing campaign depends on creative execution and the quality of the initial seeding. The online audience will pass on advertainment, not ads. Content that's funny, topical, and sexy or brings people together has the best viral currency as it reflects well on the person who relays the message, not the message originator. Many of the most successful viral marketing campaigns have come from advertisers promoting consumer packaged goods and lifestyle brands.

Tip
Design it so it appeals to the broadest range of people.

3. Run the Numbers

A viral campaign relies on a proportion of people forwarding this to a number of friends. For a campaign to be truly viral for every set of people that play in the first round there should be more people that are forwarded to and play in the second and so on. The developed strategy for a successful viral campaign will depend entirely on your objectives. It is essential to consider if you want to build awareness, create or increase a contactable customer database or even promote a competition.

Tip
Define your goal and measure against it.

4. Create Sales Opportunities

Even if it was a great viral campaign and everyone around the world viewed it - you still need to turn those views into sales. So at the end of the campaign, or ideally within it, make sure it leads to somewhere where people can buy the product.

Tip
Give them buttons to click-through to your site or vouchers to redeem in-store – let's turn the players into customers.

5. Use the Right Technology

The technology behind a campaign needs to be robust. Make sure you are doing it right. That means small file sizes; distributed servers providing bandwidth for heavy traffic or digital rights management which ensures that a campaign can only be viewed for a certain period and on specific devices. Evaluating viral spread is possible, by tracking content downloads and monitoring chart success and qualitative consumer feedback, but make sure you speak to an expert.

Tip
Load test it. How many people will it take before it stops working and how quickly can your systems scale up.

6. Reflect the Brand

Ensure the message fits with the brand's values and personality and doesn't undermine existing perceptions held by the target audience. As with any other campaign, make it relevant to the brand, otherwise you will gain little even with a successful campaign, as people are going to disassociate the campaign from the brand. Many people remember campaigns but find it hard to tell you which company it was for.

Tip
Can they tell it's your company if you removed your logo and brand colors?

7. Reward the User

What do you get for taking part? It doesn't need to be a prize but there has to be some form of reward, even if it is just an engaging animation. The campaign should deliver an online experience that stands out from the norm, offering benefits to users.

Tip
Great implementation makes for a great user experience.

8. Word of Mouse

Potential exists for exponential growth in message exposure that can far exceed what's achievable with similar budget spend on commercial media channels. Passed via peer to peer, "word of mouse" messages can help endorse a brand among like-minded consumers. Taking this non-mainstream route, a brand can be imbued with certain credibility, status and subculture currency attractive to the target audience. Include a mechanism that enables the idea to spread to other participants: Distribution needs to be part of the campaign.

Tip

At the very least have forward to a friend but how about giving them another go on the game or entry into the competition if they let you invite a friend to play.

No great viral campaign comes from an average idea. You need great ideas and great implementation. Run lots of ideas through and mark them against the above criteria and you'll have a successful viral campaign.

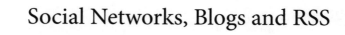

Social Networks, Blogs and RSS

Social Networks, Blogs and RSS

The rise of Social Networks, Blogs and RSS on the web has been driven by individuals feeling empowered to tell their story, communicate feelings, chronicle events or write anything that they think of. This is the age of self-publishing as never seen before and with it comes all the positives and negatives of personal opinion.

According to Metcalfe's law "the value of a network grows in proportion to the square of the number of users" which essentially means the larger the network the more connections/benefit the users get out of it.

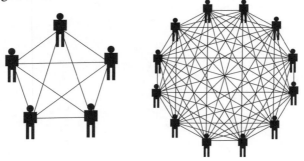

You may love the comments or hate them but with 27%[14] of internet users in the US having been involved, either reading or writing a blog, companies that ignore the messages posted may be doing so at their peril. Blogs are a valuable source of research to understand what consumers are thinking about your brand, latest advertising campaign or products/services.

A web log (blog) is a shared online journal where people can post diary entries about their personal experiences and interests. Blogs have become legitimate standard business practices and progressive marketers are building strategies around their use to influence a target audience. Many of these self-developed forums are generating significant revenue streams for their creators. Teen networks such as MySpace.com have become destinations of choice for an increasingly connected youth culture. Witness the success of Gawker.com in creating large audience pull and drawing advertisers' media dollars through the public interest in 'A' list celebrities and fashion icons. Another of growing importance is Yahoo! where they have included blogs to the search criteria within news, further highlighting the increased interest of consumer opinion, unique insights or footage of events. In addition to using blogs for research, as a feature to your site, they can increase traffic, membership and your SEO ranking. Notably in the publishing industry, we see the emergence of blogs on niche market or enthusiasts sites for example, autoexpress.co.uk.

Video logs (VBlog), are proliferating as bloggers seek to enhance their messages. Mobile blogs (Moblogs, mBlogs), can be posted directly to from your mobile communication device. Podcasting enables anyone to create their own radio or television show for download to others. And it goes on and on.

At the heart of the technical revolution in the explosion of self expression via the Web, is a family of standards called RSS and a rival specification called Atom. RSS stands for Really Simply Syndication and allows individuals or web sites to opt-in to receive content or recent changes from web sites, the most common of which are news, blogs, entertainment, and ecommerce. The technology behind RSS allows users to subscribe to web sites that provide RSS feeds or syndicated content. For the marketer, RSS will enable you to communicate and publish information that goes directly, avoiding SPAM filters, to users who choose to link to you, at a time that is convenient to them. You will be able to receive feedback on what the market would like to hear about from you and be able to widen your reach through portals like www.live.com.

Forrester outlines why marketers should experiment with RSS, especially marketers with customers who fit the profile of early RSS adopters. Even if it's something as simple as putting press releases in an RSS feed, marketers will benefit from early exposure to distributing information via RSS and receive valuable feedback from key constituents on what types of content they would like to have.[15]

Marketing and Social Networks

For marketers, do we need to know the latest on what is hot on the Social Scene and what is not? If you want to be where the audience is growing, social networks are an absolute. Public opinion is influenced there and your brand will get reviewed, praised, skewered or viral marketed to stardom.

Several ways to get started now include:

Information Blogs

Develop an information blog on your company, product or service. With approval from company leadership, communicate the latest happenings at the company, experiment with ideas and become a Thought Leader on a topic. Remember that your posts will return as other bloggers link to you and what you say is quoted in various ways. For many private companies, this is not a problem but understand that your postings can be used to support everything from contrary opinions to legal proceedings.

The benefits to this type of blogging include reaching an extended audience and in the links that will be added by other bloggers. This increases the relevancy of your site for search engine indexing.

Personal Opinion Blogs

Many top-level executives are using blogs to gain higher visibility in the marketplace. If your strategy is to build key executives' credibility so that they can be more effective in influencing the media, being invited to speaking engagements and so forth, the use of blogs is complimentary to that.

Online Advertising on Blogs and Social Networks

Advertising money is pouring into the self-publishing space. The audiences are highly segmented based on the focus of the blog. Cost for ad placement is generally lower than that of mainstream publishing sites due to the relatively new position of accepting media spends. Choosing to move your ad spend to a blog or Social Network should come under the same type of analysis as that of any other site. Refer to Rich Media and the banner advertising chapter in this book for more on online advertising.

Build Linked Blog Communities

The American political machines have been at the forefront of developing communities of linked blogs. This allows the savvy politician to create an increasingly connected constituency to state their support and drive campaign donations. Enabling your employees to develop their own site is a good way to foster a progressive culture. Ownership even within the confines of company policy still creates positive connections.

Join Social Networks

Getting involved in Social Networks has several advantages. First, it helps you understand the space and allows you to meet people who have like interests. Secondly, it enables you to influence the participants when you post your views and positions. Friendster[16], YahooGroups.com[17] or LinkedIn[18] are just one of thousands of examples of Social Networks that you can get involved with.

Enhance Messages with Vlogs

Using video and enhanced multimedia can work like TV to communicate your message. There is no medium like video for communicating emotion to the masses. Vlogs will help drive your awareness and recall to a higher level than text and flat imagery.

Podcast

Anyone with content can set up a Podcast. Just load up audio files and let people subscribe to them through an RSS feed. Podcasts are great for regularly updated content. Many radio stations are already using or experimenting with Podcast, as are many news led web sites like News.com.

Set up RSS Feeds

RSS feeds provide an easy way for companies to syndicate your content and ultimately drive more traffic to your site and increase your brand awareness. You can even set up an RSS feed for the products on your site.

Legal Issues on Publishing

Every country in the world addresses the legal issues involving public opinion. Ignorance is not a defense and when making comments publicly available, be aware that potential liability issues include among others:

- Defamation
- Intellectual Property (Copyright/Trademark)
- Trade Secret
- Publication of Private Facts

However, in the spirit of free speech across much of the world… Blog on!

Managing the Message

Is it possible to orchestrate a program aimed at influencing behavior with Social Networking and Blogging? Absolutely. Can we predict what the results will be? Probably not. Word of mouth is the most powerful factor in this medium. Bloggers are notorious for digging into the story until the truth comes out. They don't suffer lies and mistruths well and will band together to create a firestorm of unfavorable PR for those who misuse the space.

For a company wanting to build positive brand awareness, the opportunity to use these avenues of marketing is very promising. Remember that the individual rules and the power is in the hands of those who believe in your message.

Analytics for Online Marketing

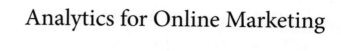

Analytics for Online Marketing

The marketing industry today is being revolutionized; consumers are being overloaded with marketing messages and have developed an increasing level of resistance to traditional forms of marketing. Organizations need to focus on marketing activities that:

1. Increase marketing ROI
2. Decrease campaign overheads
3. Maximize the lifetime value of the customer
4. Improve customers interactions with the campaign

Measuring marketing performance allows managers to focus on these activities, so it is a top priority for organizations today. In an ideal scenario, marketing managers need to know the Return On Investment (ROI) for every dollar spent, from consumers who viewed your marketing through to the customer lifetime value through every channel. Marketing managers need to have these figures at their fingertips to continue to run successful campaigns and justify their marketing budget.

There are many tools available to help you get the metrics you need, this chapter will show you which metrics you should be looking at and how to use them to increase your return on your marketing spend.

The Conversion Funnel

A conversion funnel is a metric which is commonly used to optimize ecommerce processes. It measures the ratio of customers successfully moving from step to step in the order process. Organizations have been using conversion funnels to find bottlenecks in the order process and make improvements to increase sales. Conversion funnels used for marketing need to include activities prior to the customer visiting the site. A typical conversion funnel for marketing would look like this:

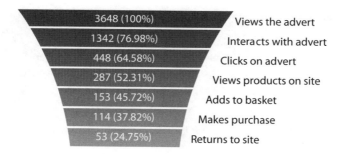

3648 (100%)	Views the advert
1342 (76.98%)	Interacts with advert
448 (64.58%)	Clicks on advert
287 (52.31%)	Views products on site
153 (45.72%)	Adds to basket
114 (37.82%)	Makes purchase
53 (24.75%)	Returns to site

At each step in the funnel, a customer can either follow on to the next step or leave the funnel altogether by navigating away. Once a conversion funnel is in place you can see which campaign is delivering the best results and feed that back so you can optimize future and existing campaigns.

Campaign Analysis

At a very basic level, organizations need to have the following real time information available at their finger tips; this will help determine which marketing methods work and which don't. At first glance this seems like a barrage of information and can be difficult to comprehend in a single take, but different sets of the collected data are required to analyze different tasks. For example, using campaign analysis to select future media properties would only require metrics on return on investment, on the other hand if you wanted to analyze which campaign delivered the best customer acquisition you would need to look at the customer metrics.

Campaign Attributes

Metric Name	Description	Example
Campaign Name	Name of the campaign that this media is associated with	KLM Come fly
Site Name	Name of the site/email list where the campaign will be delivered	New York Times
Channel	The type of media purchased e.g. email, banner etc.	Rich Media Banner
Position	Position of creative on the site	Overlay on the homepage
Reach	The number of users who will view the creative, or the impressions purchased	400,000
Demographics	The demographic profile of the consumer	Male, aged 30-40
CPM/CPR/CPC	A standard pricing metric for the media, Cost per 1000 impressions (CPM), Cost per registration (CPR) and Cost per click (CPC)	$40 CPM
Total Cost	Total cost for this site	$16,000

Campaign Metrics

Metric Name	Description	Example
Impressions Started	How many impressions started to be delivered (tracking from delivery platform)	8,500
Impressions Delivered	How many impressions were delivered (tracking on site)	8,354
Interactions	Number of interactions with the creative prior to click	435

Campaign Metrics

Metric Name	Description	Example
Clicks Delivered	The total number of clicks delivered	16,000
% Clicks	Percentage of consumers that clicked on the creative	4%
% Clicks to leads	Percentage of consumers that converted from a click to a lead	25%
% Clicks to sales	Percentage of consumers that converted from a click to a sale	8%
Number of Orders	The total number of orders generated	1,280
Number of New Customers	This is the total number of new customers	1,100
Revenue	The total generated revenue	$40,960
Profit	The profit generated	$10,200
Retention	The revenue generated from returning customers	$4,250
AOV	The average order value	$32
Lifetime value	All the revenue to date generated by the campaign	$98,630
Lifetime profit	All the profit to date generated by the campaign	$28,000
Instant ROI	The immediate return on investment	256%
Lifetime ROI	The ROI from the inception of the campaign to date.	616%
Additional stats if campaign is email based	Number of email opens, number of bounce backs and number of unsubscribed	4045 Opens 125 Hard Bounces 115 Soft Bounces 18 Unsubscribe

The information in the adjacent table forms the basic requirements to analyze your campaigns and compare sites/creative with in a campaign and across campaigns. Once you have the information, you need to look at which set of results meet your objectives. The campaign, advertising creative or site that delivers the best results, is the one to increase spend on.

A/B Testing

A/B testing is a means of testing to help improve your marketing. It allows organizations to test multiple versions of their banners, search adverts, web pages, copy, advertising placement and many other elements of marketing. Below we have outlined ways to use A/B testing to improve your campaigns:

- A/B testing is more than just testing two variations of a marketing element. It should involve multiple variations and you should run multiple iterations to find the ideal solution.

- Make a single change at a time; too many changes can lead to confusion. Take a look at the results prior to and after a change has been implemented to see if there are any improvements.

- Monitor every step of your conversion funnel during your test looking for bottlenecks. You may find a banner is generating better click-through rates, but if your web page is not able to convert, sales are unlikely to be any better.

- A/B testing is valuable when making the smallest changes, such as text size or a color change. Every item should be tested to see the difference it makes.

Using analytics to measure the results of each test you should be able to perfect your campaign prior to rolling it out. A/B testing will enable you to make accurate predictions on the outcome of your campaigns.

Improve Your Marketing

Using metrics to evolve your marketing is the only way to improve your marketing capability and your company's revenue. Analyzing your marketing activity is about monitoring three key metrics in unison:

1. **Acquisition rate** – This is the number of consumers who are attracted to your marketing activity and respond by visiting your site.

2. **Conversion rate** – The conversion rate is the proportion of acquired consumers who are converted to a buying customer.

3. **Retention rate** – The retention rate is the proportion of the existing customers who return to make an additional purchase.

If your campaigns perform well in all three metrics then you have a great formula, the key here is to continue to test a campaign until you achieve good results across all three key measurements.

The IT Element

Delivering analytics is an IT investment, the first step is selecting the right tools or set of tools to help you deliver the metrics. The next step is integrating the metric capability within your campaign and on your site.

In an ideal scenario, organizations should select a single tool that will manage all campaigns, deliver every campaign and provide analytics for all your marketing activities. This will offer a single view for all campaigns and avoid double allocation. Double allocation occurs when a single sale is recorded against multiple marketing activities such as PPC and affiliate programs therefore giving incorrect ROI information.

Tips

1. Implement tracking on all your campaigns so you know which campaign is delivering.
2. Use a single tool to manage all campaigns, deliver all your campaigns and provide analytics.
3. Every change should be minimal. Monitor the differences and the results.
4. Build up a knowledge bank of what has worked for you as you do not want to repeat the same learning curve.
5. Test, Test and Test some more.

References

References

1
May 2, 2005
US Online Marketing Forecast: 2005 To 2010 Dollars Will Follow Consumers Online, Driving Spending To $26 Billion By 2010
by Charlene Li, Shar VanBoskirk
www.forrester.com

2
IAB Internet Advertising Revenue Report
www.iab.net/resources/ad_revenue.asp

3
see reference 1

4
Hitwise
www.Hitwise.com

5
March 11, 2005
Europe's Search Engine Marketing Forecast, 2004 To 2010
by Hellen K. Omwando
www.forrester.com

6
Nielsen Norman Group published its Web Usability 2004
www.nngroup.com

7
July, 2005
comScore Media Metrix Search Engine
www.comscore.com/

July, 2005
Nielsen NetRatings Search Engine Ratings
www.netratings.com/

8
March 31, 2005
Information retrieval based on historical data
United States Patent Application 20050071741
www.uspto.gov

9
September 4, 2001
United States Patent 6,285,999
Method for node ranking in a linked database
www.uspto.gov

10
Permission Marketing
Author: Seth Godin
ISBN: 0684856360.
www.sethgodin.com/permission/

11
Internet Advertising Bureau
http://www.iab.net

12
see reference 1

13
November 4, 2005
Halloween Drives Viral Email Marketing Campaigns By Coors And Mondo Mini,
According To Nielsen//netratings
www.netratings.com

14
May/June 2005
Pew Internet & American Life Project Tracking surveys
www.pewinternet.org

15
26th July 2005
Using RSS as a Marketing Tool
by Charlene Li
www.forrester.com

16
Friendster
www.friendster.com

17
YahooGroups
groups.yahoo.com

18
LinkedIn
www.linkedin.com